Chronic Observer

poems by

Doug Stuber

Finishing Line Press
Georgetown, Kentucky

Chronic Observer

Publisher: Leah Maines

Editor: Christen Kincaid

Cover Art: Doug Stuber

Author Photo: Doug Stuber

Cover Design: Leah Huete

Printed in the USA on acid-free paper.
Order online: www.finishinglinepress.com
also available on amazon.com

Author inquiries and mail orders:
Finishing Line Press
P. O. Box 1626
Georgetown, Kentucky 40324
U. S. A.

Table of Contents

Ode to Horace Mann

Be ashamed to die until you have won some
victory for humanity. —Horace Mann

Be aware that energy is life, save some for your kids.
Be afraid that our minds are bent by news, not books.
Be awed by the healing power of the simple purple cone flower.
Be awake before the bombs drop, before the money rules.
Be agile: live in a town that walks and bikes to work and play.
Be amused by ants and birds, goats and potato fields, lilacs and sycamores.
Be angry only long enough to solve the problem, then move on.
Be ashamed to die until you have won some victory for humanity.

Carolina Wren

This time a solitary wren perches on
power lines that divide purple-blue sky,
slicing rhombi, diamonds, thin rectangles,
pushing geometry into a regular autumn
morning. This makes you wonder how birds
keep their feet warm in countries with no
power, or how people survive on a hundred
bucks a year, or where refugees go when war
hits. Our wren flies, a speck, ever smaller
as she finds her way. Given our superior
brain capacity, how is it we cause misery
across the planet while creatures so small
live, content to take their share peacefully?

Play

Brandy barks at swooping swallows,
Life, lowered to one foot or so
In summer time is simple,
As the lure of tired dogs and clover
Greets only those who need to play.

Scampering down outside stairs
Past the skidding bicycle marks
To a tumbling fit of joy
Goes the only daily memory
Of a happiness once known.

Landing in a pile of limbs,
Which includes the golden hair
That shines of wetness on the
Back of Brandy, the player
Laughs at the summer sun.

How long will it be
Before the play begins again,
Before the youthful joy
Once known appears, before
The love, if ever, returns?

Eagle Pond Farm

October in New Hampshire means colored leaves for kicking.
Donald kicks a few heading into town for cheese.
He notices that the antique dealer, once again, announced
The coming of winter by changing his sign. It now reads:
"Driveways Plowed, Reasonable Rates." The type of
De-evolution Donald appreciates.

Standard time ensures contrast, as autumn's last bonfire
Sends a leaf-shaped spark into the air.
A simple way of life is free to walk around without inspection:
So Donald does. He checks out of Najur's General Store
With Gouda and N.Y. Sharp Cheddar tucked away.
He climbs up the knoll then down the driveway to the farm.
He kicks a pinecone to the safety of the woods.
He exhales steam that quickly disappears.
He can almost see ice forming on the pond.

Room 6, Groveland Hotel

An iron door clangs,
One bat flaps over the roof
As Blythe, not snooty,
Retires after a summer-soup day.

The old jail emits the ghosts
That still haunt the top of
The hill. Imagine traveling so
Far only to be squeezed out.

Too many men, not enough
Gold, but these days, plenty
Of jails. You stake a claim,
Dig best you can, only to get

Flea bites, blisters and no
Way home after you trade
Your last mule for two
Week's slop. We don't

Know anything like that
Now. We're soft, getting
Softer every year. But bats
Flap, doors clang, and the

Flow of visitors provides
A few steady jobs. Is
This the last fling for nature?
Do we extract what we

Can and move on, or is
Our new way even more
Exploitive? Tomorrow we'll
See things we're not

Likely to see again in
This life. So here's to the

Friendly folks who spread
Joy with small porcelain

Dolls, antique surroundings,
Creative meals, funny
Ghost stories, and the humanity
To remember how it was.

Canary Row Hoe Ho

There's a hippy girl in my class who wears Mao's cap, dates
a long-haired boy and wrote a kick-ass environmental piece.
You'd like to poke through every long-leafed elephant-ear on
campus, stroking nature, this beautiful sub-plot, with hoe, adze,
al or clipper: chopping down in order to raise back up, involved
with earth as is intended. Some say a new time has come, White
Buffalo and all. Consequences outnumber rewards at a twenty to
one clip, as Mongolians suffer from bad air and China's expanding
desert, even though they've done their part to live in a preservationist
way. But global means brutal these days: global trade = wage slave,
global warming = no food, global war = death for the multitudes,
profit for the stinking rich few. Love abounds in campus towns,
while "repo-men" reap millions, and songbirds still find seeds around
as legs spread out the leaves. Our new man is African, but he is
nowhere near free, and babies laugh, and mothers smile, here in the
land of the free. So what that free means money, instead of love
and food. When no one has a dime to spare, friendship will lift
our mood. Or will there be the occasional hijacked truck or plane?
Who cares as long as we can load up the kids, drive south to live
in a genuine, warm, Steinbeck-decorated pipe that used to be a drain.

To Be Human

is to fall in love over and over,
to never give up on any of them,
to cry for the inhumanity, and try to
overcome all that surrounds us by creating
a closeness with those in proximity, both
geographical and philosophical. It is to
carry those loves in our heart, flooding our
minds no matter how gone they are. And
to put others' needs first, understand their
flaws, work on our own so we can be
better healers. It is to take it all in and
follow our dreams no matter how preposterous;
to pull apart another brown paper bag and
to write it all out, no matter how choppy.
So take my hand and make it all better
before I repeat the painful parts until
I can no longer act. To struggle past
obstructions and obligations, self-imposed and
expected; to wallow in joy, build strength and
change what we can for the better. To give.

Death Is Snow

Death is upon her. Death is persistent. Death be not
proud. Death is a series of twitches, days worth.
Death is snow. Death moans and screams. Death
is not easy, death is not random, death is not timid,
death runs on time; death hangs in the air, then
dives from on high, but not always that quick in the
suffering phase. Death is Catholic. Death is not
pretty. Death is white. Death is ginger ale, death
is dehydration, death is omniscient. Death leaves
bills to pay; death does not smile or frown. Death
is a whisper. Death comes fast for those in a hurry.
Death waits at the doorstep, greeting old friends.
Death reunites, tears asunder, acts as the final good-bye.
Death motivates. Death inspires. Death has its own terms.

Wonderment

Water rushes, tickling feet with sand.
Gilgamesh relaxes by the sea.
Purple Echinacea sends a cone into rain.
Chopin laughs and strokes his polonaise.
A beetle digs the desert, over oil.
Chang Sung-Up daubs a mystery in ink.

Water trickles down a granite wall.
Lao-Tzu hikes through summer's offerings.
Yellow lilies waver in the wind.
Tasman lacquers the last board of his keel.
Crystals mingle with Icelandic ash.
Lodi licks his chops, nudge-nudge, wink-wink.

Water batters barns from red to gray.
Burck paints Frida as Leipzig hums along.
Canandaigua feels the White Snake's breath.
Handsome Lake enjoys a drive-in movie.
Sesame rice lands in a wooden bowl.
Africa snaps a twig and starts to think.

Beauty Realized

Aspiring long-trunked Lindens
send leaf seeds spiraling
into Highland Park. The Peace Wave
dances, sings, paints, plays and eats.
A fully trimmed church social
for progressives, pot heads and artists.
Activists all.

Five women in pajamas dance
fertility, entrance patchouli-laden
jaw-dropped gawkers as their
seductive gyrations glaze
the eyes of men and women alike.
Loins slither, mingle, fling
jubilant torsos across the full stage.

Red scarves tie waists together
in a sweet maypole offering
officiated by throngs of soft naturalists.
Star city of the South nurtures
self-made lives, little cash flow
but long on love. One family fills
buckets with magnolia pods: art objects.

Now or Never

A turtle flies through the universe.
We ride on the back of the turtle.
The Undergods dwell in Canandaigua,

The Overgods look down from clouds.
Even if we're 300 moons away from
When this mattered, most of our lives

Are touched by one holy inspiration: nature.
Cosmic coincidence should not amaze here.
You are in the middle of the new awareness.

Black rocks spin and dive in deep water.
A four-year-old runs then swims.
Relaxed willow provides humid shelter.

You peek under the giant grass skirt
And see four tangled feet. You don't peek further.
Gray locusts send twirling twigs to hair.

You swim out to a cooler spot of deep water.
The white snake, awake again,
Leaves Bare Hill, not reeking havoc

But cutting new creeks to hike along,
Full of crawdads and water spiders.
You retrace ancient steps. You sneak

Through the old neighborhood, now trespassing.
Four tangled feet, a few skipping stones
And the spirit within you:

Now awareness reigns. Corn presents
A raw treat for passing minstrels. Nothing
Talked about or noticed matters.

Pablo and Max

This is the story of Pablo and Max,
They left New York City to avoid income tax
And gather some primitive artifacts.

They left in the rain in spring '52
And were seen in the fields with an African gnu
Admiring the shapes that came into view.

While Pablo was digging up red cube-like art,
Max drew some monsters on government charts.
(They looked like amoebas with elongated parts.)

The days were spent studying carvings of stone,
Or walking in jungles out on their own.
An artist knows how to survive alone.

Always popular with their new friends,
These two went about setting new trends.
They taught the natives how to pretend.

Unlike the scientists who went to steal,
The artists just borrowed that primitive feel.
A congenial arrangement, if not ideal.

Bob

More than a name, Bob is a natural mastery of life, not Jeff
or Stan, Bob is the universal sign of happiness, soul satisfaction
and Bon Ami. The ultimate adjective, Bob applies to actions,
comments, TV episodes, women and some guy's father who just
took out a copperhead by carving it up with a common shovel.
No Bob is not just handed Willy-Nilly to any passerby. Its earned
over decades of excellence. Bob is the Queen of Rock, the
Bobby Fischer, Bobby Orr, Bob Gibson, Be-Bob-A- Loo La,
Bob Hope, Billy Bob, so to be Bob, Bob Dylan your soul, curve
ball, it's you waiting to be provoked, "dotarded," if you will, five
hundred seventy feet out, out, out of Candlestick Park. Willie
is Bob. Bobbing for apples rarely rises to the level of Bob.
It depends on who's doing the bobbing, and for what kind
of apple. Bob, an anesthetic emanating from the mind, to
general surrounds. Effortless, Bob Marleys in on a wave
of half-baked brownies, revolution succeeds, life of service and
soccer: singing and dancing, that's a Bob life. So grab your
partner and dosey-doe: Bob your Bobs, let it flow. You may
know Burns, Frost, Seeger and Bobs within your midst. Stop
griping and moaning, put down your phone, stand up and be Bob.

Two needless chairs expire,

Two needless chairs expire,
Water drops on rust.
New color happens.
Man-made polyethylene lasts
While metal slowly syrups
To a puddle on cement.

The splashes splash
Much smaller in the
Thicker, sadder pool.
At the time of April
Water (loving self)
Splashes higher into water.

Needles drop on scene
On time, from pines.
Dark and bending branches
Promise further litter,
It changes green to tan
Then brown amidst the rain.

Sand is hardening, to
Become a crystal image.
Chipped-off paint adds
Yellow to a widening
Scope of dismally
Contradictory experience.

Oncebush

A oncebush, nowtwigs
Juts into the plane of
A window. Someone cut off
All the flowers, leaving
Sticks in the air.

I would have thought
This to be wise
Except that this is April.
Gray shadows interrupt
A piercing spring sun.

Spiny arms reach out
From a hanging plant.
Uneven knots combine
To hold the pot, attached
By rounded hook to roof.

Shy little light pokes
Out of the wall, its
Shadow doesn't cause a stir.
Oncebush nowtwigs solid
In its presence stays.

Atlanta

Buckhead offers twelve-dollar sandwiches,
Parents lunching their children on Saturday:
Straight from Beemer to deli to Emory to evening
Wedding to Benz to kids at lunch on Peachtree.

North Peachtree, where you can't quite see the smog
Thanks to trees and art and tacky bars. Southern
Culture on the skids, but not outside this deli, where
Leaves tumble with Dr. Brown's Cream Soda cans.

All I can think of is you: hamburgers and organic
Bananas, juices, never soda, and a complete
Satisfaction. Money doesn't earn these deli-dippers
The satisfaction you have. Inner peace even.

You cook after volunteering, after the kids are
Down for the night. You go there and back then home
To ride your bike to work. Teach me how to calm
Myself won't you? One point at five points:

There is no chemistry to teach the zen you have.
Perfect weather makes yellow leaves stand out.
Small winds coerce more travel. Sharp shadows
Waver. One beacon lures me home to paint autumn.

Lavender Tear

See if this rings a bell:
The exact feeling you have to express
Before your father dies is the one thing
The two of you never approach, so you
Go about your latest woes, or his
Beating cancer, but you can't ever say
How amazing it is that he put up with
So much for so long without raising
A peep.

Or how about this one:
Ten or twelve years into a better-than-
Average love affair you finally decide
Things couldn't be better, just in time to
Find out you don't have the balls to
Complete the function by raising some
Children. You lose her over this, and
Waste months, not sure anyone else
Will listen.

You're not sure they'll listen to the loud
Colors smacking onto canvas, or to
Bass rumblings, or some dashed-off line.

But this is a dream, and your day's night
Blends, due to insomnia. Einstein and
Zevon never slept. Broken hearts mend.

Armistice is only Words Away

Red and yellow leaves smash above remaining green
On brittle trees stressed by drought.
The fall crop grows together from fear.
War ruins the party here, starving refugees move out.

Warm sun parches grass to dust in Chapel Hill.
Light kills. News disrupts gentle walks.
Two thousand one claims close lives, no way to hide
The reign death's image starts with superficial talk.

Peaceful winds entice lovers bent on keeping war at bay.
Rice is blown to bits, extreme starvation, war means war.
The dissidents' Gulag hut awaits activist Americans,
And "your flag decal won't get you into heaven anymore." [1]

Three deer caught in lights that look like monster's eyes.
Nature, fraught with tarmac, endures another "bombs away."
Scream , young angst poets. Wipe the cynical smirk off and scream!
One life to infect your neighborhood. One chance only: today.

[1] John Prine, 1969.

Hargraves Blues

No obstacles in the physical realm can stop the
Flow of fix or ruin. One bicyclist, content to move
In limited space, dodges traffic, kicks her stand
And heads in to read. She gets paid to read, not many do.

No life is long enough to support all the relationships
We build: kids to cats, Moms to cleaning, teacher-student,
Boss to worker. One walker strides down Rosemary Street,
Pulls his hat over his ears, holds palms open, seeking change.

No gesture, however insignificant, goes unseen
In a town full of women. Drivers bounce from one plan
To another, running reds. Phone calls, calendar notes and
Breakfast fill seconds between lane changes, defying death.

No effort, regardless of intention, can sew a revolution
Without mass appeal. Two men shrug, walking into shade.
Nothing for them to do but drink and smoke and go to sleep.
The truth is here to see but no one's looking anymore.

No wind, even from Saskatchewan, can clean us now.
Some loudmouth stumbles in offering to teach, but
None will have it. A rider, bussing there and back for free,
Takes comfort when a man stands to offer her a seat.

No sandwich, ever so scrumptious, lingers past initial taste.
Sun shines on a bouncing orb. Four for four, he's another
Wizard with his hands. He does not get paid to shoot a ball.
His hand-to-eye skills have no value in this part of the world.

Corporate Suckered Us

Back when there was time, when one parent
Was always there to guide a child, schools were
Not blamed for bad behavior, partly because there
Was so much less of it. One job per house meant
Security, health insurance, a nest egg, and plenty for
Suzie to go to college on. Forget the bridge club now
Dearie, **everybody** works. Corporate has found a way
To thrive in the post-liberation era: reduce middle class
Pay to the point of nudging, nay forcing the Moms to work.
It's not about reduced free time, it's about no time left to
Even get to know our own children. Since profit is king,
The new world order is thus: No assistance if the Dad lives
With his child, No benefits to any temporary workers, No
Labor jobs that pay a living wage north of the Maquiladoras,
No wins for unions since 1980, No affordable day care
For working Moms, No federal money for states with less
Than seventy five percent of the welfare recipients working,
No job training money left after building bombs, No incentives
For employers to pay better, No company loyalty, No profit
Sharing plans, No safe pensions, No guaranteed retirement,
No Social Security, No public transportation in many
Towns, No decent schools for low-income neighborhoods,
No safeguards for the food we eat, No plan in place to
Save the environment, No cash to save the mental hospitals,
No handouts to the homeless veterans, and No jobs at all
For those who work with their hands. None, zero, zilch, zip!

Genocide, Slavery, Greed

We cry for the slavery that led to such wealth,
This is not **just** the land of the free.
We witness genocide all over this earth.
What can we do to end greed?

We cry for the land, full of modified crops
We **must** work to save human life.
What will our grandchildren have to live through
Since our appetite causes such strife?

The oil wars that started a decade ago
Have moved toward the Caspian Sea.
We are the dissidents, loud, without fear,
Even if we are cut at the knees.

We cry for the news they keep off TV,
The grapevine could snap any day.
Disinformation is the age we live in,
So who's going to show us the way?

The answer is simple, we grow as a team,
A new brotherhood in the light.
We must build the village, invite all your friends,
This is no time to give up the fight!

They have all the bombs, the juntas abound,
Monsanto is spraying the poor.
We must dig our hands into arable land
Or genetics will foul every spore.

Profit mongers have sucked the earth dry,
We must reclaim all that we can.
Industrial China, the last frontier,
Soon money will own every man.

The kids on the streets are locked-down together,
Push a bike, and you could get ten years!

All this is forced because we stopped caring,
Yet some offer blood, sweat and tears.

We couldn't stop bosses from shipping our jobs,
The replacement is for-profit jails.
Our schools are rotting, so teach if you can,
Where it counts, not Harvard or Yale.

The time is upon us, united as friends
We can make anything grow.
Come join the party, sing and dance all the day,
Tomorrow we get out the vote.

We cry for the genocide, slavery, greed
That persists after thousands of years.
It's late, but there's time, if we really work hard
We can stop the torrent of tears.

What Counts As A Life Fulfilled?

What counts as a life fulfilled?
When it takes four hours to pull your
head off the pillow, living up to ancestral
expectations is a wild dream that ends in
misery when your vision soars way beyond minor
accomplishments. Like Donald Duck, your thrusts
can be thwarted by a monk with a stick, your desire
vanquished by shutting down your entire life off
a chance meeting at a sandwich shop.

So you pull a self-proclaimed rebirth to start
the process again in an attempt to have a
career that the home-folks can cheer about.
It's a war. Normalcy versus creativity, manic
against depressed, one woman pitted against
another, and there you stand, crying, as the
police ask with whom you intend to go. You
know your insanity led to all this, so you have
to trust others to know you are on the right path.

"I accuse you of a wasted life," the judge
proclaims, and all you can do is cower and shrug
while humming Smokey's "everybody plays the fool."
It's a greedy, needy life. The path to freedom must
be in helping others. There has to be a way, no
matter how hard, to function beyond the boundaries
imposed in a bipolar way. Get out and beat back the
temptation to quit, grab the best possible offering,
count your blessings, discard the past, and proceed.

Atlas Shrugged

Lotus leaves in fountain pools behind the
Metropolitan Art Museum reflect sun rays,
but not in ways Monet would understand.
Cellos ascend to bless the ears of diners
from the donor class, while those lily pads
and lotus landings resonate on levels only
guessed at by geniuses and amateurs alike.
Room after room after room after room after
room stun mere humans with the peak
moments of nearly all the masters: ancient
relics full of universal hum. Feeling visitors
tear up, once cynical multi-cultural couples
soften in amazement. The hoity-toity mingle
with Asian tourists in a surreal scene Yves
Tanguey would get a kick out of. But it's the
quiet ripples in the pool out back, the tumbling
leaf in the now-safe park, the sad chatter
of the magnet peddler whose addiction isn't
clear, but whose profit must be small, that fill
sensory memory to capacity.

Takae

Frowsy ne'er-do-wells, agitated tennis fans, nervous
businessmen and large-rimmed ladies angle for seats
on an overbooked flight to La Guardia. Takae enjoys art,
travels from her post in Tokyo to tour the U.S., perhaps willing
to yield to a man with strong character, but not in a hurry
to give up her homeland, her dreams, her loves, or her smile.

Sewer gas diffuses from the "innocent" stitcher who claimed
the last seat on this bird full of humans, so close, but so far
apart in the way they respond to this life. Unattainable goals
rule the minds of most yankees; gold is religion, nature is
hostage. Instincts suppressed for ten generations, supplanted
by profits then cleansed every Sunday by parochial Baptists.

It's the time of starvation and gross atrocity, when
genocides play out due to no food, when clubs formed
at Yale control the whole world, when one country's
debt causes collusion resulting in deaths to thousands who
have no idea why the bombs explode. Internal resistance is
labeled "insurgent," while TVs spread lies to zombies back home.

The scuffle ends at Detroit's Metro Airport when NWA 427 finally leaves.
Precious life fades behind us no matter our fate. Takae slumbers, maybe
dreaming of Kawabata's "Snow Country" cherries, soft spring blossoms,
nature's offerings plentiful, but how many see? Our stitcher, whose
art is Santa, hollowed be thy name, thy shopping comes, thy
economy hums, the slaughtered allow all these gains.

Watercolor

Watercolors fill spaces between
Pine branches as the moon delivers
Inconsistent reflections
To a wandering man.

Winds blow, rearrange
Shadows at his feet.
This starts him thinking.
He angles across a field.

He enters darkness,
Lured by solid colors,
Wallowing away from fields
To a thick-boughed stand:

Crashes into sticky bark
Falling under weaving cones
Crumpled in a mass of blue,
Surrounded, cold, but sheltered.

We've woven a web, you and I,

We've woven a web, you and I,
attached to the world, for no matter
how long, inscribed, though poorly, for
scant eyes, still, as bright a love aura as
has ever glowed, tightly wound around
our hearts, yet soaring miles above
Moodung's fog to warm cold February.
Sparks fly off a round-rock fire rarely seen
in these parts. We laugh, it feels like we
shouldn't be here on a cold winter night,
just a few meters from trails so packed
during the day. This charge will never
leave. We've marked this space but must
go to where the stars shine, deer run, art springs.
Keep my heart in your brain, words in your hair.
Matched lifelong yearning bursts in my hand,
fluorescent. Quick, pack what you need, let's
flee! live life in the positive zone, expand
what we enjoy together, bound by the luck
that brought us this far. Where to next?

La Jolla

One Beech tree separates the cold Pacific harbor
From a lighthouse that blinks white and turquoise.
Twelve knots of wind kicks the salt up. Port lights
Warn planes, but a single starboard twice the
Width marks the length of boats passing.

Only pairs find such an April night enticing.
Earlier a rain heavied leaves that remain
From autumn. New ones stretch out to guard
Their ancestors. A few are more than one year old.

The lighthouse sends two different rays:
White glides across the ripples in a double-pump;
Turquiose snaps a single moment to sailors
Who find a type of relief in sleazy bars downtown.

Now a fog reminds the pair how eerie ports can be.
Blinking starboards try to find a place to land.
Seaplanes hangers wait for the marines to be sent in.
Chilled rocks seem immovable but they're not: newborn
Leaves of Beech know nothing of it, and should not.

Magnets Sonnet I

We sweat together like delicate chocolate.
The comfortable wrap of ancient money fails to
Freshen a purple Iris. "Would summer boil a
Luscious petal language?" "Only in Peru."

We conglomerate with threads forgetting friends.
The furniture designer conspired with unknown
Budding chiropractors. "Does singing
Interrupt suburban plight? "Only in Italy."

Let my moment whisper through the raw heaves.
The guard allows no images of love beyond
Revolving doors, demented. "Would Sitler
Score in time to save our fate?" "Only in Toronto."

We conspire against the grind, inspiring unseen art.
The joker who still wears hats all year round
Inspires another line: no hate. "Does smelling
Take the place like food of touch?" "Only in Peru."

We sweat together like delicate chocolate.
"Would summer boil a luscious petal language?"

James Of Manning, South Carolina

I'll bet you think the caste system
Is reserved for India or the far east,
But what of the American man
Who volunteers to sweep

The butts and trash you throw away
From the sidewalks and lots:
Then he comes inside to ask if
You can spare a fiver from the slot.

Of course you can't but you
Give him a hot cup and he goes away.
Which he does because there are
Other lots to sweep today.

I'll bet you think your job is safe
Handing out donuts, coffee and tea.
It's not if the boss across the street
Picks a foreign locality.

And what of the man who sweeps so well
And his kids who he never sees?
Do you ever stop to think or tell
Of his life of misery?

Donuts, Not Manna

Chafed red hands dangle under
A dungaree coat. Faded threads
Except for purple lettering: Camel.
This dude's a mechanic, works fifty
Hours under cars. He's never read a poem.

The scowl of poverty greets you
From a face, still beautiful, behind
Blonde hair. She decides she can't
Afford a donut and walks out without
A morsel, without a sip, without a poem.

Is there poetry in the wind shaken
Locust trees? Maybe behind the
Wheel of an F-250? No. You
Can't blame words for hiding. This
Isn't the right era to sit writing lines.

Can anyone drag a poem out of fake
Wood paneling on a rusting family
Wagon? Is there any beauty at all
In the design made by cracking
Blacktop? Words like people cower.

War Sonnet

Bombs float gently, flaking off occasionally
In the wind, disrupting well-planned patterns.
Mountains (being less populated)
Miss the worst attacks.

Snow is far too soft to bear the brunt
Of ugly metal. Generals forget this,
But soldiers seldom do. Red on white
Creates a gloomy contrast.

Frozen memories never thaw,
They stay cold until reality has changed.
Forgotten joy is hapless against the night,
Unrecognizably split into microscopic pieces.

Tracks lead in but never out:
Angry men cuss their lonely lot.

Tragedy At Woodside

The Millhopper puffs
An ethereal mist into the night.
Insects forget the danger
And come on six point landings:
Secure at Dali Memorial.

Ants and uncles wait
Inside the terminal, protected
From the memory of fright.
Most are happy in art's custody
But one takes off, quite unsatisfied.

Screams of horror beg
Her not to go, but youthful instincts
Coax her to greater heights.
She clears the creek heading over trees,
Landing lightly under Gala's brush.

Corkscrew Swamp

Blue Heron walks on Lettuce Lake.
Lily pads support light birds long enough
For them to bill crawdads. Appetizing
Photograph: Squirming crustacean crunched.

Boards, cleverly cut, fan out around corners
That bring new cypress vistas into view.
One tree grows around another, wet but
Not waterlogged. Raccoon poop, which has

Red dots throughout, brightens the walk
As rain clouds defy winter and roll
Through desolate Florida. Where are all
These cars going? Immokolee?   Must be

A growing town to support such traffic.
Back at the swamp a frog succumbs to a
Banded owl. Anhingas stretch wet wings.
White flowers waver, waiting to be painted.

No Boundaries, 2001

Gayle paints poems in the butterfly breeze. Two boats
Shimmer in the morning sun. Evalyn drops in. . . to clouds forming
On the western bank. Last night a raccoon scurried. One deer,
Off the hill, looked, charged and jumped onto the dunes.
Dan has walked this circle thirty times, reminding materialist
Watchers that creation comes, shovel in hand, not from
Piling up, but tamping down. Seeds fall out of him,
Drop to the sand, coagulate, dry up and cause a laugh.

Imagine the control it takes to let it drop without the squirt
Of normal urgings. (It takes more control to deny the gifts: to
Match philosophies—divine.) So we march in happy paradise,
Using wits to develop efficiencies that will give our kids
A choice: more freedom means more obligation, but how do
You get that through to Johnny sixpack? Where is Jarrie
Going to sit: among the quintessential consumers, or
Back in a cabin, using little energy, but commanding

Electric friends via concepts and inventions so compelling
That, just like Curried Einstein, the tide runs toward new
Shores? Days go by like blinks, Gayle ponders how
Much longer this slice will go, but she knows her
Evolution is many lives away. Entangled souls expressing
Love's constant yearning gather on this sunny island as
Wind and water wash it all away. Robert, stick in hand,
Walks back and forth, waiting for the change that starts it all again.

Fayetteville Mall, September 5, 2002

In the shade across from the Wake County Courthouse
An entire row of folks wait. They wait anticipating
The crown-stripped Miss North Carolina, and others.
"Mary," who carries a baseball bat, handcuffs, and
Thirty bracelets, watches as the Capital's finest walk
The worn out bricks of Fayetteville Street Mall.
The thick stench of racism pollutes beautiful fall air.
Sympathetic eyes search for compassion as workers
Dismantle metal scaffolding, a job well done. Lily pads
Float, bald-headed briefcase toter huffs and puffs up nine
Stairs. Sturdy capitalists go by: easy targets. Unaware.
A local high princess displays her hair seriously. Orange
Outfits mix with cell phones, coffee and power lunches.
No rich people come out of the court losers, but many
Weeping wives head back to Person Street frustrated
By a system gone awry. They too are easy targets.

Dharma

Moth eggs attached to rice in a bag.
Illusions of movement where reflections hit black.
Quartz clicks like water torture.
Veins pump half way:
Clogged by clots that are one inch away
From stopping tomorrow from becoming today.

Baby black toads hide in mulch.
Beetles eat magnolia blossoms.
Wind dries droplets formed on plush leaves.
Rain clouds hover:
Change from dark gray to black.
Erosion, the first sign of entropic attack.

Alive, tan moth flutters, a simple life,
Seeking refuge in fabric or candles by night.
All is one and one from the all:
Since, from this earth all life uncoils,
If unconnected, all life is spoiled.

At The Mill

Soft Shenandoah shelters misfits and malcontents,
nurtures sheep with large genitals, photographer's family,
hay-hoisting horse owners, trick-turning truck stoppers,
inventive harvesters, Steeles Tavern sewers, bountiful beauty.

Naturally, writers abound surrounded by such: one wins
five grand at the pharmacy, takes leave of the women
long enough to type her new voice, a beacon who
fortifies fellow polygamists with purple-winked ink.

Fur-clad apparition returns, disrupts midday bushwhack
with its presence, historical, ominous, predictor of days
you can't bear to ponder. Satiated, you grab her hand
for emotional balance, slipping down moss-laden rocks, afraid.

Grinder-switch melodies follow tight patterns until, fed
by grain, new grist emerges. Wind spirit magnifies terror;
your steps quicken, but you think of three others: photographer,
writer, compost collector: a post coital spook, still yearning.

Tang Quest

Red morning wind kicks
leaves over vegetable cage.
Felled white oak patiently
absorbs blade after blade.

Chunked wood magically
stacks upon self, against mud.
Sawdust darkens. Winter rain
slows work, allows love time.

Pond refills, frightened turtle
relaxes. Cool December water
welcomes geese and herons
to rolling clay-built hills.

Man and woman join; new
child cries, coos, sleeps.
Six point buck stops, observes,
moves slowly out of view.

Fog lifts, sun creeps past
logs, warms three thousand
trees, sixty moons past white
buffalo's birth. Bonus time.

II

Colorful turkeys gather
under lit moon; feathers
diffract beams to cedars
lined, two rows; historical
trees whose dead branches
dangle predictions at pond's
edge. Three run to flight,
circle, drop back, contrive,
spread; anticipate coming of

spring. Winter rain cuts fog.
Hilltop oaks sparkle when
wind pushes limbs through
ethereal mist sent down to
visit this New year's Eve.

III

Hair-bellied bull
stands. Dainty tied-foot
girl spreads parasol.
Protrusion emerges from
hair; pillow placed,
dress-becomes-blanket;
fantasy or farm boy
hovers, slogs. Heavy
mud slows progress.
Results equal effort:
parasol quivers, wind
stiffens, girl rolls, wakes
inner spirit, follows
heart-made trail
to pastoral life.

IV

Respected grandfather ties
green maple branches,
nails joints, rakes
leaves onto compost,
works tools vigorously,
reads after dinner,
speaks less than one
paragraph per day.
He is bent over:
seventy-eight years
translating, teaching, gardening.

Happiness, not out of reach,
but produced by
simple living.

V

Watching ladybugs,
tuning to zen movement,
could transform one
overindulged son-in-law.
First he must learn to
separate men's and women's
tasks, no easy lesson
for western man.

Down By The River

Black juice squirts and spills, dirties your day-old shirt
in time to impress the bag-boy at the "Korea Town Galleria,"
which is kind of like a flea market plus basement grocery
store located in the heart of neighborhood number four.
Number one being Watts, number two is Compton, three
is East LA, and then Koreaville, just south or north of
Wilshire, but miles apart, with bullet proof cages in liquor
stores, security guards in lots already valet attended, and
a weird mix of fleeing Koreans, homeless Caucasians, slow
moving Mexicans, and scary impoverished wide-eyed
urbanites. So many trade blooming persimmons, the comfort
of sameness, and bad air for this: wilting Oleanders, racial
inequality, and the same traffic jam, same air, same struggle
to pay high rent, but now in neighborhoods you wouldn't
walk around in day or night. Open lots as garbage dumps,
freeway madness, and the unobliged rich cordoned off
in Bel Air. Let's say, for giggles, some do give a hoot,
they then gather their friends and pass turkeys to appreciative
but suspicious arms on Thanksgiving. Great, but that leaves
a lot of days left, and since government is not in the business
of helping anyone but business, who will clean up the lots,
make jobs that pay well, create block parties where the four
main sub-groups actually enjoy commingling? Sandy Sierras
poke pyramids up from desert dunes strolled by the ghosts of
Bukowski, Zappa and Steinbeck. Neil Young hangs on, but
once he is gone, the entire hope that flickered when Vietnam
ended will have been dashed. If you're not sad yet, wait 'til
the market crashes and the chaos begins down by the river.

Hikaru

One cherry blossom detaches, falls, a single unit
allowing fruit its space, starting its new journey: island
to reflecting pond, orchard to cottage yard, daughter to
lover, enhanced by the wind, if even for only six seconds.
Transformed to long-boned genius, long-yearning adult,
considerate friend, purple-green plaid from soft pink,
tan suede boots from four-petalled bloom. Hikaru, as they
say in Japan, hits the town running, arms crossed, cradling
herself like the war-torn victims of Vietnam, but not
worn or torn, she flings enthusiastic youth toward
outstretched limbs. She captures her beginning and future
simultaneously, shedding one form, embracing another,
sweating humid Spring, still awkward in this skin.
Descending unannounced, she moves among mere mortals
spreading joy, quietly demanding obedience, offering all
in exchange for all. Most cannot accept, choose an
easier, less complicated path; but those brave strong souls
born from deep roots, blessed metamorphosed
beings who join Miss Cherry soon realize, if for one day,
week, or lifetime, their lives will never be the same

Play II, Thirty Five Years Later

There's this shadow made by Korean Pines that hits
the white wall of building two at one every day.
If you're sitting upstairs at An Die Musik, lazily
waiting for your favorite lunch-mate, this shadow can
appear to be the cliff seen in ancient watercolors. A
dark cliff and foggy white air in a far-distant place.
Foreground cloud-clipped conifers add a touch of reality,
nudging you back to lunch, which arrives, unlike your partner.
Today it's the newfound cliff, visible only from three
southeast-facing seats. Students move, shoes push grains
into jagged cracks, yellow buds enlarge, the sun warms
frosted souls, but it's the shadow cliff that matters. Now
you have a new friend, silent but hopeful, strong yet fake,
everlasting but ever-changing, finally receding with the sun
to a place no one knows. A morose quartet, early romantic,
pops at least one bright piano note, while cello, violin, viola
continue their lament. A new banner is stretched between
trees. The perpetrators are efficient and mingle into passersby
in less than thirty seconds. Now the cliff cascades, trios walk
and talk, you dream of love alone, confident it will return.

Unnamed University, Unnamed City, Unnamed Woman

She lies back, angel wings spread, feet flat, but
arched back allowing head to inhabit old-school gas
oven. Mouth open, nostrils flared, deep inhale is more
than photo-op, it's real, she's forever shamed her family
by laying drunk as 18 fellow classmen raped her. Every
person in this town knows what happened, but she is the
one who must take her life to balance family sadness, apply
guilt to those who just avoided jail time conventionally.
Here, where rules so outdated they make the Catholics
look hip, her family will not pursue the raging animals
who committed this atrocity, instead they'll be consoled
by funeral guests, and their money. According to the
Confucian beliefs (held more dear in Korea than China
these days by a long shot) it would be harder for her
family to go on if she was alive to tell the story.
You don't have to cry about this, many already have.
These "men" walk free to start university life, having
completed "Membership Training," the custom in which
families pay extra for weekend retreats and the school
sanctions and organizes: alcohol, food, pajamas, rape?

We don't

sit in a parlor, harmonizing, conducted
in on cue to solo over the top,
nor bump the snow off dark branches
only to ruin the soft-edged contrast.
We don't know anything of traipsing the
woods for love, skiing three miles
cross country to peek at the town beauty
working out, unaware, glistening, another
Cynthia Brewster or flower-sniff come
spring among thick rushes, floating above a
rocky bottom pond, water so clear you drink
as you swim, laughing, naked, holding back
nothing, calm, sitting one branch up the
plum tree, white-blossomed. Careful now, do
not adore her too quickly or she'll think you are
weak. We don't know naturally how diverse
life interacts, lavender and finch, smiling
girl and chrysalis, no, we've allowed ourselves
to be penned in, self-domesticated via
electricity and cars. Come love, let's walk.

Truffaut here
means movies, booze, a
quiet respite, candlelight
and real jazz though not
a "jazz" bar.

Here, a "jazz bar" is
one tender
per male patron; they
offer mostly talk and peanuts,
no music.

Thunder skies
wake adults: children
do not hear, nor frequent bars
this side of downtown.
Truffaut rules.

Musicians start or
end nights here,
the truly hip find
nooks to plan clandestine trysts,
or gossip.

Time dissolves
under piano riffs,
sax wailing,
conducive to heart
calls, so couples come.

A sip of
Baileys on the rocks, better
here: life fades,
deep meditation
for us lost drunk souls.

Zen Dye, Sendai, Send Die

Throat swells, gums bleed, lymphs bulge on and off in this
post-nuclear tsunami Asian spring with its radio-rain and
sadness because years of stress already determined most people's
cause of death, but now it's a relative surety that cancer rates
will fly five years hence. Sixteen students sweat a mid-term,
young enough to never have imagined life-shortening storm,
still sure the orgasmic joy of youth will last forever, or at least
looking forward to blissful mating, large alcohol, unflinching
prosperity and a good job awaiting stellar grade point average
in a system where a B+ is a slap in the face. Stress exudes
and clogs up the aisles with a goo so sticky it's hard to collect
the exams. So Bright smiles, scores well, heads to a mid-term
a scant 10-minutes removed but ever so cheerful, even if she
is truly so embarrassed about leaving her pencil case behind.
Living proof that life goes merrily along amid the worst type
of disasters: corporate (Tepco shouldn't have allowed tons
of radioactivity to spread into the Pacific), financial (banks
got trillions, sold homes at 70% off, foreclosed 9000 per day,
then asked for more bailouts), governmental (fascism at every
turn), environmental (look at it all, and still we drive our cars).

Saint Valentine pulls
flowers from
his frock. Do all saints
wear monk's clothes? Here's to Mom's our
working saints.

I love you,
though my mouth causes
huge rifts, please stay close now.
Our nation of three
remains strong.

Since love conquers all
allow this
small ink flow to wash
past agony away. Your
heart needs me.

Busy life
leaves short hours to be
alone with you, but your heart
beats inside mine all
day and night.

Let the smiles
return, let me support your
art, teach my
slice of the world to
Hyuntay, our hero.

Take clues from
him, the son who asks questions,
the light that
brings us together
with daily magic.

The Springs

Let's go down to the springs,
We can watch the dogwoods grow.
Let's go down and watch things,
Get up right now, let's go!

The water will be running,
We certainly won't miss that.
Today you do look stunning,
Let's go down and chat.

There's something I want to tell you
There's something I want to say:
Now we're a nation of two
Starting this very day.

So, let's go down to the springs
We can watch the dogwood grow.
We'll hear the bird that sings,
There's one thing that I know.

When we go down to the springs
We'll see if two can be one.
We'll avoid the things that sting
And catch a little sun.

The thing that I have found
Is a love for only you.
My heart will always pound
When I enter our nation of two.

This Woman Walks

This woman walks, sunlit floodlight drains
energy, on. A crow signals all-clear, so she
swings the carved sign, ignores the jutting roof,
opens heart, he's back. Fieldstone chimney:
historic tug floats out from its cabin,
angled shadow balanced by conifer gargoyles is
spring. She hears beauty again.

Wind waves
long-leafed dandelion
into white azalea.

The Falls

Broken fender, twig in line
And light blue sky with trees.
Green on blue and mountain fine
With warmth upon my knees.

Summer sun at winter time,
Snow still on the ground.
The place is set for water-mime
So I listen for the sound.

The sound is one of Bash Bish Falls
And now I tend to stare.
Everflowing echo calls
Of water in the air.

It makes me think of trees gone by
And people never seen.
It shouldn't, but it makes me cry
To think of where I've been.

Now I sit with tears on face,
Knowing all the glory.
Now I sit without a trace
Of how to tell the story.

Nine Slapper

Blue bird in the air,
Golden boy delights.
Skipping stones without a care,
Singing in the night.

Seagull pierces silence,
The dawn is on the rise.
Fishermen are busy
Watching for red skies.

River wanders, digging earth
Fertilizing soil.
Weekend mongers slobber
Spilling pints of oil.

Red-skinned native stands,
A reminder of the past.
Spearing fish and digging clams,
Hoping they will last.

Blue-eyed boy walks on,
Determined to have fun.
Lonely lovers cry,
Searching for the sun.

Once, when I spilled,
   No one cared.
      (The cleaning was so simple.)

            Imagine the tender
            Thoughts that evolved
            From an experience unseen.
            Feel with me
            What I felt that day.
            Share, if you can
               (with me)
            What I have done,
            What you have done.
            An experience
               (of)
            Our own, to own forever.
            Eachness into a
            Oneness of unseen . . .

Now, when I spill,
Someone cares.
(The cleaning was so simple once.)

There, in the bush
At the hill
Under leaves
Was,
On this blue
And often hazy day,

A soft reflection of you.
Memories of the times
(few of them ever knew)
A slender subtle line.

A curved, not bumpy rock
Apparently not hard.
It came as quite a shock
To find the grain so sharp.

So, there, in that second,
While it lasted
In its warmth,
I,
At that moment
Loved you.

We Won't Wait

Seven slimy salamands
Go crawling off the wall.
Thirty watching whippoorwills
Chirp a warning call.
Threatening mist diffuses downward.

Nine abandoned bugs
Wish the water well.
Many mashed mosquitoes
Are on their way to hell.
Summer rain causes quick changes.

The lizard and the flower
Soak the water then:
New insect generations
Needn't wonder when.
Notice the rapid revolutions.

Five frightened philosophers
Grasp at things the same.
Knowing nothing is,
No one near to blame.
Changes catch clumsy lovers.

Eleven laughing lizards
Know that this is true,
Fortunately, my love,
You now know it too:
Affection can not afford to wait.

The Mangrove Blues

The sun sinks.
A pumping heron
Chases dreams into the night,
Resting momentarily
In a life of constant motion.

The wind shakes.
Trees stretch out,
Anticipating winter.
Orange floods
Mangroves and the pines.

The cold turns.
Clouds gather
Over murky surroundings,
Drifting slowly inland
To dump a fresh-new load.

The tears run.
A skipping child
Delivers momentary reprieve.
Gloom infests
The evening of a lonely-hearted man.

Morning—Farmhouse

This place has contrast:
Not just the greens either.
Fog settles on a backdrop
Causing Kentucky Blue to melt in
Behind the bright trees of Virginia.

Assorted cows meander
Into the Tolkien postcard-picture,
Dotting hills with slow sienna.
Hearing makes its way
Past the primal sense. Shapes evolve.

Singing birds. Hark, spring.
Rain underscores with the
Power of timpani.
The creaking house stirs, cats claw
At what is left of the upholstery.

The coolness of the brick
Shelters wanderers from humidity.
White sheep jump the cattle guard
To graze on the yard: love is
Staccato in the overture of morning.

Eye-Level: Stack D, Library East

"Where is everybody?" asked the voyeur, not above suspicion.
"A mile beyond the moon" replied the Georgia boy.
"She was a billion dollar sure thing, not like other girls.

I wanted to take her down the thruway to Wonderland:
An encounter in Key West with the old man and the sea.
There is so little time in the lives of girls and women."

"Life is life," said the Georgia boy, "winner take nothing."
"I heard the general zapped an angel,
Turned her into Kentucky ham, a real Roman holiday."

"I have so little time (87 days) to find the crossroads
Out in mumbo jumbo. I'll steal the smuggler's bible
And find the sneaky people by following the curve of the snowflake."

"Listen to the whispers of the player piano,
Take five smooth stones from Deep River,
Remember, sleep is for the rich, and don't forget
The protocol for a kidnapping," the mutant advised.

So off I went on a couch trip in search of a hero.
Across the river and into the trees,
Determined to be home before dark.

Suddenly, in the air, she appeared, the wine of life,
Sam's legacy, a small success, exclaiming:
"While still we live, let no man write my epitaph!"

New Potato

Just what are we supposed to
Accomplish
In this leftover culture?
Apathy soup or
Mindless decadence? Meatloaf or gold?

Start modern traditions now.
Discover
Potential by ignoring
Everything they want.
Play hard then dedicate completely.

Jump off, get straight, share yourself.
Initiate
New dances for the timid.
Create vibrant space
And keep the space open to change.

Publicize your ideas.
Saturate
Your neighborhood with abstract
Lifestyles made of art.
Drop the past like a hot potato.

Water

One more walk, rain, walk
But this time the sprinklers that
Never stop watering sidewalks
Stop. Eight hundred fifty seven
Trips by these sprinklers, which
Water the sidewalks at a school
That, moneyless, blows $85 M
Per annum on Public Relations and
Administration, finally yields a view
Of recalcitrance: black tubes
Back into the earth in the middle
Of a rain. It doesn't stop blonde
Hair from being tossed back, or
Bikes from hitting pedestrians, or
Green sports coats, yellow ties from
Entering business classes. But the hope
That one day someone will shut
Off the lights at the pool glimmers
In the minds of the living.

II

No Bananafishing today J.D.
Just another scrap of laughter
In the middle of one hundred
Days-in-a-row of living death.
Almost no one is right anymore.
Money is the orgasm, orgasms
Are inhibited by AIDS, AIDS
Keeps the population down un-
Naturally, so why go to war?
War feeds the rich, the rich feed
Themselves. Hockey players buy
Raytheon, Raytheon builds Patriots,
Patriots kill when ordered to
But feel bad when they realize
A hundred thousand "men-in-sheets"

Running away have been shot down.
Bush buries a dog that died
From drinking water that never
Became a priority on Capitol Hill.

III

Blue is no longer good enough
To squelch the ugly feelings
That persist through fog's insistence
In the pastoral green suburbs of
Alachua County Florida. Services
To farmers will now be discontinued
As the city merges outward to
Expand its fading tax base. The
Poor, if they are downtown, will
Not get better schooling because
The real problem, of course, is law
And order. The recent (1990)
Attempts to form gestapos have
Only been denied by the narrowest
Of margins. Barbara, your husband
Is a fascist. So please don't drink
The water, unless it's jugged in
Plastic which keeps the Exxon
Floating down a waterway near you.

IV

Execution replaces caring in
Societies gone mad, where the
Idea of rehabilitation threatens to
Take away the jobs of racist police
Pretenders who offer few excuses
For their deeds, so often brutal.
But if L.A. and Miami think the
Problem is lack of order, wait 'til

They find themselves without drinking
Water. The business of water is
Clearly Canadian, a group that owns
The rights to sell, in moderation,
Water from the north. For now its
Fancy Cola, but soon this rare
Commodity will falsify A. Smith.
Chicago will have it listed on the
B.O.E., and drinkers everywhere
Will be beholden, as farmers
Are today, to the trading pits.

V

The light gray elm remaining
Is dark, it rains today.
Smug tie-dyed pseudo-philosophers
Prance in the warmth of winter,
Believeing nature's last gasp a fun
Time. Explain why cars get less
Than 100 MPG. Explain why trains
Have been usurped by trucks and
Japanese MPVs. Listen to yourself
Justify the oil glut and go off
To die for someone else's greed,
As the shinning path demolishes
One more village while quick
Decisions earn millions in less
Than pristine Salomon accounts.
How do you like the fact that
Everything's a lie? "The battle is not
Between Democracy and Communism,
But Democracy and Capitalism."

VI

Here, at the school where once

Every six years the sprinklers go
Off, you can get suspended for
Practicing the right to free speech:
Expelled for persisting to do so.
The idea that a university would
Founder free-thinking is too much
Under the mercury umbrella of
Late-century conservatism. If
Water makes it to 2050 then
Jump for joy and laugh at the
Whining contained herein. But
Don't expect all-correcting nature
To save it for you. The idea of
Bringing children into this is repulsive.
Save your relationships some other way!
When water prices fluctuate at the
Whim of investors, you'll see how
Dear the price of living can get.

Peering Out Fish Windows

Just when your life is reduced to a gray squirrel,
Syncopated , hopping from one nut to another,
Tail waving on a jolting body,
You're trapped behind fish windows.

Exactly when the wind stops,
When joining trees and bushes in celebration
Is your natural reaction to the beauty,
You can only peer at what is real.

When the sun hits, when predatory birds
Stain cold mountain with dark shadows
You're stuck. Stuck behind fish windows
In man-made air on naugahyde furniture.

Just when you could be one with it all
You stop. Unable to fulfill desire,
You conjure a scene. It's you, throwing stale bread
To a squirrel out, out beyond fish windows.

Fish Windows Number Two

This view of frosted Tinker,
Fabled mountain, accentuates
Streams of winter clouds floating
In the season's lightest blue.

Drooping, thinning, browning pine
Initiates surprised walkers
With the season's final droppings:
Clumps of snow, impotent cones.

Eighteen leaves and forty-five pods
Shimmy, unwilling to take
Wind's frozen ride on ice.
Hanging on to life too long.

This view, barren foreground trees
Towering over frozen cliffs
Terrorizing passing clouds
With piercing arms, is winter.

Fish Window Number Three

Nothing moves fast in two-degree weather.
Snow stops, grass browns, trees creak.
A dangling pod denies an entire generation.
Five-step cloud lingers a quarter hour.

Fish window isn't wide enough to see,
Isn't Tall enough to breathe, isn't old
Enough to feel it in its joints. But, a
Camouflaged manhole cover steams.

Two yonder trees make visible
Ten thick branches, contrasting light blue
Frozen sky. A silver tag twitches.
The active agent is two degrees.

One (it will be dead for three months) bush
Absorbs the manhole's offerings quietly.

Fish Window Number Four

Old Harry the heron walked right up
And put his beak on the plexiglass and looked in.
We've got special plexiglass here,
It'd take a bull to break through this stuff.
Harry's been poking his neck around Lake Lorraine
A couple of weeks now. He seems depressed.
They wouldn't want us to get out, or hurt somebody
To hurt "ourselves." That's what the codes are for
Harry looks like he lost a friend. Wish I could
Tell him everything will be all right come summer.
These codes are "A," "E," and "S": Assault, Escape
Or Suicidal. If you get a code you're in but good.
Harry's working his way toward "S" code now
Stumblin' around like that. He better not let 'em see him.
Down here's the ICU, intensive therapy, no privacy.
We're in a circle: beds in little slices of a pie.
Once in a while harry will come by or the tree frogs'll
Yelp all night making the natural nuts go off.
The nurses can sit doing their books and see
All of us at the same time. You don't dare beat it.
If they knew Harry felt the way he does, they'd lock him in,
Restrict him from minnows and make him express his loss.
Just the other day, I got me a big "B" code.
Now I can use the bathroom alone. You know what that means.
Harry better stay away from the lake. It's so tempting though.
He's got to grow up and tough it out a few months, then summer.
Big John lets you shower as long as you want, so I wait for
The 4 to 12 shift before I go in. Big John Laughs.
From my slice you can see Harry out on Lake Lorraine.
I stole some foil to try to catch his eye, but I missed him. Lake
Lorraine is a horseshoe pond made when they dug up some land
To use as fill when they built C-2 and C-3. If you're a good boy
You get to move up to C-2 where, once-a-week you leave the
Grounds to go shopping. They wouldn't want you to lose your
Knack for shopping. Guess they figure $70,000 a year means
You've got to re-learn how to shop. Shows you how much
Freud knows. But for the natural nuts it's a big deal.

Leaving the grounds means giving up security they tell me.
I don't believe them. I piss and moan, when asked, about
How long you can lock someone up behind fish windows,
Legally, without that person having done so much as spit.
They say I've got to stay until I'm well. Well, anyway, I'm stuck
Behind fish windows for life. I'm stuck, but look, here's Harry,
Strolling along, wagging his neck, tapping fish window number four.

Fish Window Number Six

Not moon pies and a blue RC, instead a purple LSD;
I look for streaking gerbils in the snow,
Find green sprite cans scattered two-three-four:

Below a turning Z-car one demises.
I come, escaping truth, for one more fling,
Find long hairs frozen, broken off by sweat.

I come, like Gala Dali's mind, in blue.
A breasticle of liquid, propped by crutch.
Expecting snow (like flakes) to pound again,

A Douglas wiggles windy under insulated rain:
A Scottish botanist traveled overseas,
In search of fir, not nether fur you see.

I search for feelings in a desert-brain.
Douglas never had to search so far.

Fish Window Number Seven

Ever seen a willow in winter?
Scraggly horizontal branches
Dangle thin stirrups swaying
Against gray sky.

Wind pushes them diagonal:
The uncut tail
Behind a wild horse:
A wild horse charging.

Or a long-hair
Walking quickly,
Attacked head-on
By the same wind.

Fish Window Number Eight
(Save us Jimmy B.)

My life is trick upon myself.
A dead bird fell from the sky.

Jimmy B. jogged up a hill
In yellow,
Pushed through tree branches
And hugged a girl with
A ghetto blaster in her hand.

Is this how birds die?
I thought,
One last fling across the sky
Only to drop like a rock
Into the shade of fish windows?

How can Jimmy B. jog by
And let this type of stuff happen?

Fish Window Number Nine

Yellow springs early,
A bowl of charity ill-received.

Blue waddles in,
Dashing antique hopes.

Faith knits a shawl
In time to wrap granny before she . . .

Red violates distinctly,
An accomplished linear distraction.

Green surrounds serenely
Launching puff-balls to a dream.

Jimmy B. remembers
Not to somersault in public,

It being spring.

Barbee-Sue

I sit in Barbee House unnoticed,
Uninvited, a mason jar full
To overflowing: crushed ice: an
Original wild berry flavored cooler.

I write, as the jar, wrapped in
A torn brown once-bag.
As the felt on the bag,
Exuding red water-soluble ink.

It rains. This disappears before you
Read it, and I, the lone alumnus
In this alumnae building, flow
Onto a white manicured davenport.

Then, as sweat pours down my
Hot-humid epidermis of glass
I stop enough to gulp myself
Before the last drop hits the floor.

Soup Is Good Food

Coffee grounds, like so much weeping,
Never find a place. You can't fertilize with tears,
You can't exasperate yourself with leftovers.

Eggshells, like so much death,
Have no place thinking. You can't explain their existence,
You dare not whisper in their presence.

Fifties decor, like so much sex,
Never adds to the place. You keep your condoms
Hoping to avoid disease. Never get a chance.

Kodachrome, like so much tax,
Places judgment on obstacles. You grind
Existence into death, snapping housefly moments.

Banana peels, like so much emotion,
Send ball lightning through your place.
Nothing grabs like solo meatloaf dinners.

Rules

It took this long to hide my penchant: Rhymes.
Another reading forces inner looks.
Where is Ed and his heroic Elegy for us?
What happened when we traded love of lines
For time cards, bosses, corporate crooks?

Here's what happened: life became a chore,
There is no time left to rage creating.
Competitive suburban gardening is a bust.
What there is left is not elating
Except the love of soul-mates through this door.

The Eagle's Nest is now a restaurant:
You get a 15-dollar turkey-plate up there.
But is a fourth Reich rising from the rust,
Or are we evil, just nonchalant?
Oklahoma City fades like sunset air:

The only lasting image is your own.
One veto and the fascists will shut us down.
One thousand points of veto from the upper crust
Without a batted eyelash from this clown.
What further outrage can we condone?

As long as TV says it is OK
Our lives submit to the worst human rages.
Just when we've farmed this place to dust
Some half-assed savior might come our way
Passing manna to those left: food of the ages.

The Shining Path

Plant technicians spray
Untold zillions of hanging and or
Boxed flora. Oxygen-producing takes on new
Importance in buildings where windows
Only open text.

That someone might need
Fresh air, never occurred to design
Teams hired to assist architects who sealed us in.
So a whole generation gathers,
Squirts, fertilizes.

Job-production, an
Old game with a new twist, keeps just
Enough folks working to avoid revolution.
The illuminati keep us all
In place 'til needed.

One day the flower
Box jobs may disappear. The meek may
Inherit what is left after the "enlightened"
Have gobbled all the rest. For now:
Dig, spray, replace, dig.

Oxford Commons Remain

Ten years later, it hasn't changed:
A few small cafes with hippy sippers.
Punks have added youthful spirit,
But their unwashed brothers
"Fight for peace" then smash bike riders,
Not keeping the spirit once conceived.

Belinda carries special feelings,
Treat her well, but expect great things.
Do not let her off so lightly,
Keep her moving in the green.
Keep in her path and learn to listen,
She is aware, her path is clean.

Be all you can be, work for peace,
But brothers don't go smashing heads.
Sit on cemented blocks, rousted nightly
By the city's finest: blue patrol
With walking sticks. Belinda ducks
Such foolish swings, not smiling.

Listen to the drunken minstrel,
Laugh when selfish people enter.
Gather, but don't stay too long.
Grab a hunk of what is needed
Then spread the word amongst the young.
Knowledge kept is shameless greed.

Settle for no less than perfect,
Develop space that is your own.
Keep that which puts asunder
Violent trends within your group.
Let the mean boys wander off,
Become the village of your dreams.

KC and the Thanksgiving Prayer

I gave a thanksgiving prayer to a new family I met near Asheville.
I got twigs and built a triangle (the three goddesses: corn, squash and
beans) and a square (the four directions: North - Winter and cleansing,
East: Spring and beginnings, South: Summer and warmth, West: Fall
and remembrances. The triangle sits above the square, because it is the
goddesses who feed us: corn, squash and beans.

You start in the square facing West and, while turning right for each
new direction, say:

We salute you for your wind and fresh new sky
We salute your wonderful people and cleansing snow
We greet the day with dreams to labor by
We salute your sun and love and fun and go

To green mountains, cold river by the leaves
Of Rhododendron bushes, tall black trees.
A new friend of mine now believes,
Captured by spirits she feels and doesn't have to see.

Six PM, 25 December, 2001

It is her birthday, still she works
The wok, offering noodles, broccoli,
Special home-baked Christmas cookies
Brought to the table in a plaid tin.

Ruskin, home of the traveling tomato,
Plays host to a broad cross-section
Of Christmas diners. No Tet here. An
Eight-pack multi-generation family walks in.

Spanish and Chinese attempt to communicate
In English. Three couples in a row
Pick up take out. Over 60, loneliness
Screams from behind steaming plastic lenses.

Intermingled fortunes make her wonder
What the next customer will want.
You can't believe everything you eat,
But we know crunchy veggies cleanse.

The dog and the dragon do not always get along.
She says thank you so much as she accepts
A three-song CD gift from a strange man,
Now done eating, looking to make a call.

Hard working Spanish-speaking revelers
Eat Chinese for Christmas dinner. She
Points to a pay phone, so the dog and dragon
Talk, then drive away from the vacant mall.

Each Day Complete Now
6 January, 2002, #4

Yellow springs to red:
Three week beard bristles under
Turtle-brass glasses.
Heaving chest attests to valiant days
Spent loving life, yet
Yearning for another shot.
Each day complete now.

Tufted gulls scream out:
"My food not yours." New chicks chirp
In Palms, aware that Mom
Has won again, enough to feed them.
The clank of dredge barge
Snaps thoughts back to you, brother.
Each day complete now.

Blue, gray, white, unite
At constant horizon, soft
Even liquid here
On the patio, never the same,
Tears ever present,
The years flip by like pages past,
Each day complete now.

Mr. Chan At A Country Club

Fluid Tai Chi graces the corner of one normally
Barren parking lot. Patience meets balance as this
Cool October morning warms up. Suddenly the
Peacock explodes from the crane, a leg snap warms
Circulation, then back to slow motion: we don't
Know this speed here. When did we start to lose
Our connection to nature? Fourteen geese squawk,
Rising sun angles on to windshields as breakfast
Seminar munchers file toward a boring but essential
Presentation. Once you have your place in the world,
You have to attend all kinds of meetings. Success is
Relative in this lot, but Mr. Chan does not stay long
Enough to counter the flow of parochial greed mongers.

One Love

Last night I left the Cutlass convertible running
In the cold outside a motel in Roanoke, Virginia.
It was a dream, so somehow the next morning
The proud red touring car was still running.
There was confusion: one car too many, one to
Give away, yet we ended up walking to the top
Of Buck Mountain. Tad, who visits my brain
Via songs, was clutching his chest, asking to walk
Slower, so we stopped. A master woodworker
Had carved stairs and banister out of Curly Maple,
Black Walnut and Oak. Tad and I, exhausted,
But happy, sat kicking pebbles, reminiscing about
Lacrosse games, various concerts and the incredible
Women we had known. Then U-2 came blaring
With their classic "One Love" and I woke up,
Quickly realizing that he managed to hug me
From heaven with a song. I scurry to the phone
To see if everyone who knew him is still OK.

For Lenette

Big Ed of Big Ed's drives a big Hummer now.
Down-home antique kitchen supplies hang over
serious conversations: it's interracial in a downtown
southern redneck way. Walked by this place seven
years without stopping in. Eight waitresses smoke,
waiting for the lunch crowd. A forty-year-old with
tight braids down her T-shirt, bouncing horse-like
in the light that pushes between moving legs, and
customers who openly defy non-existent tobacco
ordinances too, but no one cares or notices except the
pen-pusher plonked in the corner. Braided lady
adjusts her chest by loosening her shirt from her
pants. Does it matter that some pretentious wanna-be
from the factory is more proud of his security badge
than a Cherokee warrior would be, returning from battle
victorious? Big Ed's sign says, "no checks, no credit
cards," hence the Hummer. What matters here is a
respite for the homeless. A five dollar warm up
in January, full of info, like "it'll be fifteen minutes
before we start lunch, you want to wait?" Yep, he'll
sit in a comfortable chair, pondering how to spend
street-hustled change for some time before deciding
what to eat. Gentle respect and hard work gain large
nods from the spirits floating in bedecked open rafters.

Weaver Street at 15

Dark-rimmed Carrboronians use muscular
hands to lift and twirl hair in a rain-soaked
morning that leaves moms and kids bewildered.
Over organic oatmeal, Mexican scrambled eggs,
home fries and humus, conversations fly from
clear-cut developments, to eight shades of green,
to upcoming Reiki sessions. Which parts of today
will be remembered tomorrow to tell red-heads
surrounded by admirers, or lost friends waving to
your inner landscape? What about his latest bout
of ego-fusion: cacophonous mumblings accented
by the hysterical giggle of eureka-struck feminists.
Arch-backed stretching maneuvers surface to
draw your eye away from a stunning new arrival.
She gets up, snickering, as soon as the pony-tailed
Latin Studies T. A. approaches the last chair.
Outside the eating end of Weaver Street Market
our red-head now walks a young Siberian Husky.
The post-graduate table fills up, and one last
"wow" of approval wafts back amid "ciao" and
"buh-byes." A budding socialist smiles, confident.

(T.A. = Teaching Assistant)

Words

Words succumb, now a vital tool of the right.
The appropriation was immediate and complete.
The guardians of left wing philosophy took a day
off, and Zinn and Chomsky excepted, watched,
as words jumped ship. Now piped into the head
of the masses in ways too numerous to squeeze
into even the breadth of a poem.

Caterpillar

Over fifty scraps lie scattered across from the mission
and Salvation Army in Raleigh's Moore Square. A cop
on horseback does not pick up. A skinny man heads
west on Person, his shoulder bag is a red square around
a black square. The nautical flag for hurricanes comes to
mind, as Mrs. Miller's fourth grade runs a Frisbee relay, ten
yards removed from the daily horrors of homelessness. Now
Norm, purple-shirted attendant, starts to sweep trash, dump
trash, and greet the park's residents with a cheery "good morning."
It's 40 ounces, a Newport pack, toothpaste boxes, Styrofoam
cups. "It's messier than usual today," he gimps on his way to
another litter zone. Miller's museum magnet kids are already
back inside when three empty school busses and an empty
trolley motor past. This reminds you of the sixty busses you saw
parked under water in New Orleans, and the white cops who
wouldn't let black residents flee Katrina's flood, and the
traumatic gait Norm still succumbs to while picking up trash,
and the four-year-old boy holding the bottle that feeds his baby
sister, and the sign at Denny's offering a chance to contribute to
the hurricane fund, and the caterpillar currently crawling up your
leg, just needing a friend. You remove another caterpillar, the wind
gusts, and another man in purple walks through Oak's mud, backpack
full to brimming, striding quickly, nowhere to go. Brown caterpillar returns
for a third visit. "What makes me so special?" I think, rising to leave.

KV, Jr.

The world's a lesser place today,
my friend Kurt has passed away.
He wrote of one-foot pubic hairs,
monkey house, foma, atomic glares.
Each time a deer comes through our yard
I see one fenced in Kurt's canard.
One May at Hobart's graduation
he told parents, in his estimation
they had wasted their hard-earned dough
by allowing their spoiled children to go
to a school more like a holding tank
where beavers opened and drunkards drank.
He did not expect to be invited back,
but the cap-robed kids had laugh attacks.
With Kurt and Molly Ivins gone,
who's left to light up things gone wrong?
Who will publish, who will read
the next attack on corporate greed?
Who will stand, sing and holler
about the way they spend tax dollars?
Bokononism lights a fire in sand,
foot to foot, hand in hand,
after Ice-Nine depletes the earth
of all its water, little mirth,
except to sit and masturbate,
everyone dead from one mistake.
The marines were tired of getting wet,
Time to re-read Vonnegut.

Yobo

She's in a biopsy now. A Mike Pease print of the
Mohawk Valley hangs out here, waiting to be
recognized as Upstate New York via only red barn,
trees and moraine-built hills, left behind when ice
caused the river. Finger Lakes just southwest from
his well-made snippet, the fifty-eighth of one hundred
twenty. Pease is good, but not good enough to keep
my mind off Yobo's procedure, no less results, and the
road ahead. She's scared, visibly scared, even a tear
in her eye, but this needs to be a no-stress day, so I
excuse myself between ultrasound and biopsy, allowing
that leaving creates more nervousness for Park, not the
type that cottons to surgery of any kind. This room has
folks from Danville, my matriarchal great-grandmother's
home. This and the print nurse me through this time. A
quick run over to return a brace-shop miss-mailing keeps
the innards from churning. Now laughter flows through
the room full of cancer patients and their supporters.
Yobo's late now, in overtime on the biopsy table, with
Doctor Chong overseeing an Indian intern. He's got
trachea, arteries and lymph nodes to miss, and whew, he
did miss, so here she is, ice-packed throat, alive, but upset.

No Bees, No Honey, No Apples

A wagon wheel of discontent
hangs from the rafters above
a stark white room where people swoon,
but rarely fall in love.

A drenching rain flows past dead grass
on land scorched from global heat.
A Heron chick wades in a pond
no deeper than her feet.

A farmer trims the pond-edge growth,
but gets his tractor stuck in mud.
Neighbors store great gobs of art
that once hit Berlin with a thud.

A liar squawks from a studio box
at W-A-M-U.
Diane responds, in quivering voice,
"How can you say that Stu?!?"

A multitude swarms the streets,
many without regret:
economics, home to roost,
in the land of war and debt.

A singer sings, arms hiding breasts,
but otherwise she's bare.
Selling sex far easier than
selling songs that dare.

A worker trapped by bills and mate
has nothing but beer and TV.
Wagon wheel turns as Iraqis cry out,
heartbroken refugees.

Pittsford, N.Y. Meets Gwangju, R.O.K.

It's amazing how hard bakers work, the way trumpets still
blow jazz, the interplay between street peddlers and birds, the
look on the face of the young couples strolling the day after
their first night together, the hundreds of tornadoes that
visit the U.S. in this, the time of global disaster on a
multiply-local scale, the softness of a plaid velour shirt over
terrycloth sweats and flip flops on a comfortable woman
who can move slow in a world so fast palm sized computers
can't keep up. Even one square meter of shade is sought
on a 20-minute walk in this heat. The shady side of the street
defies Johnny Mercer era, attracting everyone once summer
hits. Sincerity, so hard to find in the info-overloaded now, is
natural in Gwangju, Korea, the city that suffered for the cause
of democracy, only to see its fate pushed down repeatedly by
elected officials who ignore the fact that their seats in power
were enabled by the very place they withdraw funding from.
It's why laughs and friendship last forever here, why it
reminds you of your grandmother's four-mile walk to teach
in a one-room schoolhouse, or Uncle Ken's Pharmacy/Mayor
combo back when he knew everyone's prescription and name.

Acknowledgements

Ode to Horace Mann   Hazmat Review Vol. 7, Issue 2 (2004):
Carolina Wren
Play   Obelisk, St. Petersburg Junior College, 1980
Eagle Pond Farm   Mangrove Review University of Florida (1984-85):
Room 6, Groveland Hotel
Canary Row Hoe Ho   Poems from the Heron Clan V (2018)
To Be Human
Death Is Snow   Top Secrets, Open Secrets, Chonnam University Press, 2013
Wonderment   Poems from the Heron Clan II (2005)
Beauty Realized   Poems from the Heron Clan II (2005)
Now or Never   Poems from the Heron Clan I, Katherine James Books, (1999)
Pablo and Max   Obelisk, St. Petersburg Junior College, 1980
Bob
Two needless chair expire   Obelisk, St. Petersburg Junior College, 1980
Oncebush   Obelisk, St. Petersburg Junior College, 1980
Atlanta
Lavender Tear
Armistice Is Only Words Away   "Poets For Peace," Chapel Hill Press, 2002
Hargraves Blues   Poems from the Heron Clan II Katherine James Books 2005
Corporate Suckered Us   Poems from the Heron Clan II Katherine James Books 2005
Genocide, Slavery Greed   Poems from the Heron Clan II Katherine James Books 2005
What Counts As A Life Fulfilled   Poems from the Heron Clan II Katherine James Books 2005
Atlas Shrugged   Poems from the Heron Clan II Katherine James Books 2005
Takae   Poems from the Heron Clan II Katherine James Books 2005
Watercolor
We've woven a web,   Poems from the Heron Clan III Katherine James Books, 2015
La Jolla
Magnets Sonnet
James of Manning, South Carolina
Donuts Not Manna   Hazmat Review Vol. 2, #1 (1997)
War Sonnet
Tragedy At Woodside   Obelisk, St. Petersburg Junior College, 1980
Corkscrew Swamp   Poems from the Heron Clan I, 1999, Katherine James Books
No Boundaries, 2001   Poems from the Heron Clan II (2005) Katherine James Books
Fayetteville Mall, September 5, 2002 Poems from the Heron Clan II (2005) Katherine James Books
Dharma
At The Mill
Tang Quest
Down By The River
Hikaru
Play II (35 Years Later)
Unnamed University, Unnamed City, Unnamed Woman
We don't
Truffault here
Zen Dye, Sendai, Send Die

Doug Stuber is a poet, artist and retired professor living in Chapel Hill, NC. He founded Poems from the Heron Clan with Ed Lyons and Richard Smyth in 1999. He holds a BS in journalism from the University of Florida, and an MA in English, creative writing, from Hollins. His work has appeared in *HazMat Review, Kakalak, Mangrove Review, The Road Not Taken, AIM Magazine, The Obelisk* and others.
www.dougstuber.wordpress.com   kjamesbooks@gmail.com

www.ingramcontent.com/pod-product-compliance
Lightning Source LLC
Chambersburg PA
CBHW021151090426
42740CB00008B/1045